P9-CLC-310

The terrible and wonderful reasons why I run long distances

The **terrible** and **wonderful** reasons why I run long distances

The Oatmeal

Andrews McMeel
Publishing

Kansas City · Sydney · London

Table of contents

Nearly a decade ago,
I started running.

It began with short little jogs, and then I moved on to
5ks, 10ks, half marathons, full marathons, triathlons, and eventually

ultra marathons.

In 2011 I ran my first ultra, and it was a 50 mile mountain run
with a total elevation change of 17,400 feet. My toenails fell off,
I lost seven pounds in a day, and it took eleven hours.

For me, running has always been a meditative act;
when I run, I think. Most of my comics are written in my
head while running, so it suffices to say that running an
eleven hour race in addition to the days, months, and years
of training that preceded it afforded me plenty of time to
take a hard, honest look at *why* I run. These thoughts
ultimately culminated into this comic.

So without further ado, I present:

The terrible & Wonderful reasons why I run long distances

Part 1. The Blerch

Marathon runners often describe a phenomenon known as "hitting the wall."

They refer to "the wall" as the point in a race when they feel physically and emotionally defeated.

I do not believe in the wall.

I believe in The Blerch.

The Blerch is a fat little cherub who follows me when I run.

He is a wretched, lazy beast.

Slow down, Captain SpeedyPants!
Let's go home! We've got gRavy to eat and naps to conqueR!
Also, the Robocop tRilogy on Netflix isn't gonna watch itself.

He tells me to slow down,

to walk,

to quit.

"Blerch" is the sound food makes when it is squeezed from a tube.

"Blerch" is the shape of my tummy after a huge meal.

If I am sedentary at a time when I have zero excuse for being sedentary, I call this "blerching."

The Blerch represents all forms of gluttony, apathy, and indifference that plague my life.

I grew up a fat kid,
and in a way The Blerch is my former self.

13

I run because I'm terrified of becoming that kid again.

I run because it's the only way
I know how to quiet the monster.

I run because, deep down,

I *am* The Blerch.

Part 2. The ~~Eating~~ Feeding

There is a stereotype that if you're a runner, you're the type of person who celebrates ALL forms of healthy living.

I AM FRIGHTENINGLY PASSIONATE ABOUT

SPINACH SALADS!

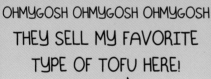

OHMYGOSH OHMYGOSH OHMYGOSH
THEY SELL MY FAVORITE TYPE OF TOFU HERE!

HIGH FIVES FOR PORTION CONTROL!

HECK YES I DID NOT EAT TO THE POINT OF VOMITING!

I am not that type of person.

They say you should treat your body like a temple.

I treat mine like a fast-moving dumpster.

My feeding habits are that of a trained circus animal: every time I do a trick, I get a reward.

It's awful.
It's unhealthy.
It frightens the elderly.

But I take no joy in dieting.

Running through forests and over mountains and under massive cityscapes makes me feel ALIVE.

Eating iceberg lettuce and counting calories makes me feel tired and robotic.

19

I run long distances for the **worst** possible reason:
I run to eat.

I punish my body outdoors to
atone for my atrocities indoors.

Seriously?! Gladiator AGAIN?!
Also, I *really* don't think it's good
for you to keep eating like that.

NONSENSE!
I RAN TWENTY MILES TODAY!

nutella

I know I should stop,

but I'm not going to.

Part 3. Selfishness and Krakens

You know how it feels after you pay your bills,
catch up on email,
and clean the entire house?

I love that feeling.
I strive for that idyllic nirvana.

Ahhhhhhh.
I am in control of my life and
all is right with the world.

The problem is

I don't like paying my bills,
I find replying to emails to be cumbersome,
and I hate cleaning the house.

I like to skip all that crap and go
straight to the nirvana part.

Running is a magical shortcut to that euphoria.

It enables me to feel like my life is **rocketing skyward,** even if it's going straight to hell.

But in reality, what did I ACTUALLY accomplish?

I shuffled, groaned, and sweated over a 26.2 mile stretch of pavement before gorging myself on granola bars and passing out in the warm afterglow of a runner's high.

HOP!

I run long distances because it makes *me* feel better.

I run because I want to slay the Kraken;
I just don't want to actually lift the sword.

Part 4. Vanity

"I read somewhere...
how important it is in life not necessarily
to **be** strong, but to *feel* strong...
to measure yourself at least once."

- Christopher McCandless

from Jon Krakauer's *Into the Wild*

Running is not about vanity.

If I wanted to look good I'd get a gym membership and stand in front of a mirror doing bicep curls.

I'd go tanning and drink protein shakes and participate in all the other synchronized stupidity that has come to embody **bad gym culture.**

Take, for example, **stomach crunches:**

Crunches are an exercise where you lie on your back and angrily try to head-butt your crotch.

HRNG FTHIP HUNGF! I'M GONNA SMASH YOU, PENIS!

HRGUHHMPF! I HATE YOU SO BAD, VAGINA! GOTTA SQUISH YOU!

They're uncomfortable, bad for your back, they do nothing for your core, and they're purely **vanity-driven:** people only do crunches because they want six pack abs.

(Never mind the fact that even if you do ten million crunches a day, you'll never see your abs unless you diet like crazy and drop your body fat percentage.)

But people do them anyway. They line up on the gym floor and pound away at their privates like frantic little hamsters.

HRGF!

SO MAD!

UNGFUHHH!

CRUSH THAT CROTCH! UNGRF!

These are the same people who read beauty magazines while jogging on ellipticals and drinking Diet Coke.
They wax their chests and wear stupidly tight muscle shirts and painfully obsess over all the superficial details of the fragile little carbon-based-meat-suitcases known as their BODIES.

Unless I wear v-necks, people will think I'm old.

I feel less whole without makeup on.

These types of people also tend to spend a lot of time lying down in these things:

If you are considering entering a tanning bed, I have some advice for you:

Do not fall into this thing.

Fall into something *real* instead.

Fall into a good book.

Fall in love.

Fall out of love.

Fall into a hole.

Fall into something.

Fall into ANYTHING of consequence.

Just don't fall into a tanning bed.

These machines are for vapid, narcissistic idiots who have barren vacuums where their thoughts, fears, and passions should be.

Spending time in a tanning bed will only earn you the appearance and intellect of an inbred baked potato.

Don't be a baked potato.
Be a person.

Narcissistic baked potatoes are the antithesis of why I run.

Running is not about building strength
and wearing it like a fashion statement.

It's about finding strength
and *measuring* yourself every single day.

I run long distances to *feel* good,
not to *look* good.

I run long distances because I am not,
nor shall I ever be, a baked potato.

PLEASE ...
JUST SOME TRAIL MIX...
ANYTHING!

Part 5. The Agony

One of the most
terrible and **wonderful**
runs of my life happened several years ago in Japan.

It was hot: 104° Fahrenheit (40°C) with full humidity.

I was running up a mountain that was nestled against
a large city, and, because of the intense heat,
this mountain was completely devoid of hikers

—so I was alone.

I'd been running for hours, and my GPS watch told me
that I was seventeen miles in.
I hadn't brought enough water, and I was
hot, tired, and dehydrated.

Everything hurt.
My muscles screamed.
My skin seared and blistered.

Even my BONES seemed to ache.

At the base of this mountain was a massive bamboo forest which, although beautiful, was home to an army of **Japanese giant hornets.**

Japanese people call these hornets *Oo-Suzumebachi* (オオスズメバチ) which translates to "Giant Sparrow Bees," due to the fact that they're huge—almost the size of your thumb.

These hornets have stingers which are 1/4" long (6.25 mm) and can deliver venom that melts human flesh. The sting, which is considered to be one of the most painful on earth, is so bad it'll put you in the hospital.

On average, Japanese giant hornets kill 40 people a year, making them the most lethal animal in the country.

Point is: I *really* didn't want to get stung by one of these monsters, which groaned by every few minutes like Luftwaffe dogfighters.

BEEP!

PERSONAL RECORD ALERT!
Congrats!
You just ran your
fastest mile EVER!

Heat. Agony. Dehydration. Hornets.

These were the thoughts that plagued me during the run.

I was too hot and miserable to enjoy the run

physically, and I was too worried about the

hornets to enjoy the run emotionally.

But that's how it goes with runners: through pain, we find serenity.

The greater the agony, the greater our eventual absolution.

The vending machine sprung out of the side of a hill where the forest gave way to city.

And within this vending machine laid an arsenal of sugary, satiating beverages.

I chose a purple one.

KA-THUNK!

There are few experiences in this life which I would describe as religious.

This purple drink was one of them.

It tasted like the **souls** of
ten thousand unborn panda bears.

It tasted like someone stole the balls off a
pegasus and blended them into a smoothie.

It tasted like sugar, water, and absolution.

It tasted good.

Part 6. The Void

REBORN

from the enchantment of my grape beverage,

I took off into the forest once again,

and as I made my way back up the mountain,
the weather began to change.

The sky blackened,

the temperature dropped,

the wind roared,

and the bamboo trees began to CRASH into each other

groaning and snapping and wailing in agony.

Lightning **exploded** over the treetops,

and rain began to fall.

The hornets fled the forest,

and that kingdom of heat and worry and torment

which had belonged to those nightmare insects

became a kingdom of **bliss,** which belonged to **me.**

So I kept running.

It was on this day,
during this terrible and wonderful run,
that a thought occurred to me,
a thought which has never left me:

I've always considered *the* question to be

"Why am I alive? Why am I here?
What's the point of *me*?"

And to that I say:

WHO CARES!
FORGET THE *WHY*.

YOU ARE IN A RAGING FOREST
FULL OF BEAUTY AND AGONY AND
MAGICAL GRAPEY BEVERAGES AND
LIGHTNING STORMS AND DEMON BEES.

THIS IS BETTER
THAN THE *WHY*.

I run because I seek that clarity.

Maybe it's superficial.

Maybe it's just adrenaline and endorphins
and serotonin flooding my brain.

But I don't care.

I run very fast because I desperately want to stand very still.

I run to seek a void.

The world around me is so very, very loud.

It begs me
to slow down,

This 36 footer is a real beauty, and it's guaranteed to NEVER play TV shows that challenge your intellect, EVER.

SALE!

to sit down,

Introducing ...

facebook
for your FACE!

I like it!

to lie down.

BLERCHHHHₙ!

Finally ...
a recliner so comfortable,
YOU'LL DIE IN IT!
FINANCING OPTIONS AVAILABLE!

And the buzzing roar of the world is nothing
compared to the noise inside my head.
I'm an introspective person,
and sometimes I think too much,
about my job and about my life.

I feed an army of pointless, bantering demons.

Hey, Remember that time you did that thing
you were ashamed of? No?
Allow me to remind you for no reason!

I'm going to recite this list of items that you
have absolutely no control over,
but you should worry about anyway.

Every single thing you do in your life,
somebody else is doing a better version of it.

Hey, your demons are a bunch of jerks!
Forget those guys ...
let's eat this entire cake instead!

But when I run, the world grows quiet.

Demons are forgotten,

Krakens are slain,

and Blerches are silenced.

THE END.

In the previous chapter, I mentioned being chased by Japanese giant hornets. For the sake of brevity, I left out a rather interesting tidbit about the dynamic that exists between these awful hornets and their not-nearly-so-awful cousin:

the Japanese honeybee.

So, in the name of science, I am happy to present:

A TOTALLY UNNECESSARY DIGRESSION ABOUT

JAPANESE GIANT HORNETS!

When European honeybees are exposed to Japanese giant hornets, it does not end well for the bees.

A single Japanese giant hornet can kill an average of forty European honeybees a minute,

→ (That's one corpse every 1.5 seconds.)

and a group of thirty can wipe out a colony of 10,000 European honeybees in an hour.

WHERE IS YOUR GOD NOW?!!

BOOT!

This is because European honeybees did not evolve alongside Japanese hornets, and therefore have no natural defense against them. *Japanese* honeybees, however, have had OCEANS of time to deal with these flesh-melting, nightmarish creatures, and have evolved a very unique way of combating them.

When a hornet nears their nest, Japanese honeybees will swarm the hornet and enclose it in a tight ball.

The honeybees will then vibrate their wings, which turns the "bee ball" into a convection oven.

Japanese honeybees can survive in temperatures of up to 122°F (50 C), but a Japanese giant hornet can only withstand temperatures of up to 115°F (46 C),

So, the honeybees will raise the internal temperature of the ball to exactly 117°F (47 C),

Hornet
Honeybees

110F   115F   120F   125F

thereby roasting the hornet to death,
but leaving themselves unscathed.

Isn't nature neat?

The DOs and DO NOTs
of running your first
MARATHON.

DO let those pre-race jitters fly!

Start out at a completely impractical pace.
This will demoralize other runners into quitting early,
and you will be crowned marathon champion at mile two.

DO NOT stop running when getting a drink at an aid station.

By enduring the "sprint-choke," you could shave three, possibly four seconds off your 5+ hour finish time!

Remember:

marathon success does not come from training or perseverance,

it comes from waterboarding yourself at aid stations.

DO over-accessorize.

Because you're totally gonna need all that shit.

DO NOT dwell on those who are clearly doing much better than you are.

For they will only drain your life force.

WEEEEEE!
Running is great.

Shoes are great! *I* am great! JOIN ME! Let us run together, for we shall talk about many wondrous things, such as sunsets and yogurt and autumn foliage!

INSTEAD focus on those who are clearly in hell.

I call these people "springboards."

K ..KKK KK... KILL MMM ...MM...MMEEEE.

WOOOO! I'M FEELING SUPER! Outta the way, Mr. SadPants!

SHOOM!

DO NOT remind yourself
that you paid good money for this.

marathon: *(noun)*

A popular form of overpriced torture wherein participants wake up at ass-o-clock in the morning and stand in the freezing cold until it's time to run, at which point they miserably trot for a god-awful interval of time that could be better spent sleeping in and/or consuming large quantities of beer and cupcakes.

See also: masochism, awfulness, "a bunch of bullshit," boob-chafing, cupcake deprivation therapy.

DO NOT despair

when thinking about how much farther you have to go.
Instead, console yourself by inventing
bizarre ways of measuring distances.

Hey, only eleven miles left! That's like four loops around that park near my house. I run that loop all the time! **Eleven miles is EASY!**

I once heard that Godzilla's penis was roughly three miles long, so this is like running lengthwise down a couple of Godzilla wieners.

This is no problem. Piece of cake.

Yessir, it's gonna take a lot more than a couple of floppy lizard penises to stop me. Everything is going to be okay.

I am going to be okay.

DO end on a high note.

When you see the finish line,
start sprinting like a coked-out orangutan.

No one will ever suspect that you walk-jogged the previous 26 miles.

HRNGGH!!!

✓ **DO** hang out in the recovery area and chat up the happiest bunch of physically battered people you'll ever meet.

✓ **DO** ignore all the warning signs that something horribly traumatic has just happened to your body.

✓ **DO** forget every single second of agony, frustration, and melancholy that plagued you over the past few hours.

✓ **DO** this with food in your face and a gleam in your eye.

✓ **DO** all of these things,

and then go enthusiastically sign up for another race.

Same time next year?

ROGER THAT, GOOD BUDDY.

Hate the outdoors?
SO DO WE!

There are beavers and pine cones and a bunch of other crazy bullshit.

With the AssCore 9000, you can safely exercise indoors while catching up on bad television!

100% fewer beavers, pine cones, and life experiences, <u>GUARANTEED!</u>

ORDER NOW

and we'll throw in a FREE DVD featuring 14 hours of gerbils running in elliptical patterns.

BONUS!

A LITTLE PERSPECTIVE FROM A LOT OF GERBILS

The Blerch's guide to dieting.

You're a RUNNER. You need CARBS. Carbs get converted into glycogen and will give you energy during a long run.

Oh, well in that case I guess I could heat up some brown rice and broccol-

Brown rice? NONSENSE!

SLAP!

Well, do you think maybe I should go for a run after this?

A RUN? NONSENSE! You're tapering for your next big race.

But that's like five months awa-

NONSENSE! You're a champ, and a champ needs his rest.

At the gym:

who is looking at whom.

The Lean

I wish I had gimungus meaty muscles like that guy. I bet girls line up around the block to gargle his privates.

LOG OUT,

POWER DOWN,

AND GET THAT SCREEN
OUT OF YOUR FACE.

GO OUTDOORS,

EXPERIENCE THE WORLD,

RIGHT NOW.

UNLESS IT'S COLD OUT,
THEN FUCK THAT SHIT.

WHAT AM I? A POLAR BEAR?

IT'S HOT CHOCOLATE TIME,
MOTHERFUCKER.

A conversation with my taste buds.

THERE'S NO RUSH.
HAVE A SNACK INSTEAD.
MAYBE A NAP, TOO.
SERIOUSLY, JUST TAKE IT EASY.
TAKE A LOAD OFF, BUDDY.
YOU EARNED IT.
EAT THE WHOLE CAKE.
EAT THE WHOLE GODDAMNED THING.

Things that make me run fast.

1. ~~Seeing an inspirational sign.~~ NOPE.

2. ~~Being told that if I sped up just a bit, I might set a new personal record.~~ NOPE AGAIN.

A lazy cartoonist's guide to becoming a

runner

Many years ago, I found myself working a job where I was
spending seventy hour weeks in front of a computer.
Morning, noon, and night I was firmly planted on my butt,
absorbed in a realm of slouching, snacking, clicking, and typing.
After several years of this, I noticed that my body had begun
to take on the shape of an overweight tyrannosaur.

Always thinking about snacks.

Tiny, pointless arms.

T-REX

ME

90% of body weight located in
the thighs and buttocks.

At first, this was okay.
I didn't mind a growing resemblance
to my Cretaceous doppelgänger.

What began to bother me, however, was that I was spending my entire life staring into glowing plastic boxes all day.

So, on one chilly spring evening of no particular consequence, I went for a run.

I didn't get far. I hadn't exercised in years so I could only go for a few minutes.

The next day I ran again,

and I was able to make it a little bit farther.
The day after that I ran almost a mile,
and the day after that I ran OVER a mile.

This pattern continued, day after day, week after week,
and within a few months I'd lost nearly 40 pounds,
dropped three pant sizes, and outpaced one
very cumbersome dinosaur.

I did not become a runner to lose weight,
I did it to escape my computer.

I started running to *feel* better, not to *look* better,
and I have created this guide with that philosophy in mind.

This is not a step by step guide to drastically losing weight or
getting six pack abs or completing a marathon.
It's a collection of things I did to make running *stick*.

Think of it as a deranged, rambling meditation from one
former T-rex to another.

Some of it isn't pretty,
and some of it isn't for everyone,
but it's what worked for me.

1. Shut up and *run.*

You'll never run out of reasons to take it easy. Your brain, body, and circumstances are all working around the clock to convince you to sit comfortably on those marvelous bum-cushions of yours.

" The weather sucks today."

"I'm slightly sleepier than usual."

"I worked out really hard the other day, so today I'll just take it easy."

" My favorite running socks are super stinky."

" I'll start exercising on Monday. Mondays are better for forming new habits."

" That squirrel in the front yard is really mean and scary."

If you find yourself debating whether or not
you should go exercise,
it means you have the time and the means,
you're simply talking yourself out of
doing something difficult.

DO NOT participate in this debate.
Do not engage that apathetic little beast.
Don't even look him in the eye.
It's an argument you're going to lose.

Just put your shoes on and GET OUTSIDE.

Pretend your butt cheeks are a pair of cruise missiles.

Cruise missiles are meant to be launched.

They were destined to CRUISE, SOAR, AND OBLITERATE.

And that's exactly what you're doing.
This is outright war against a bottomless supply of excuses.
It is a blitzkrieg of the buttocks.

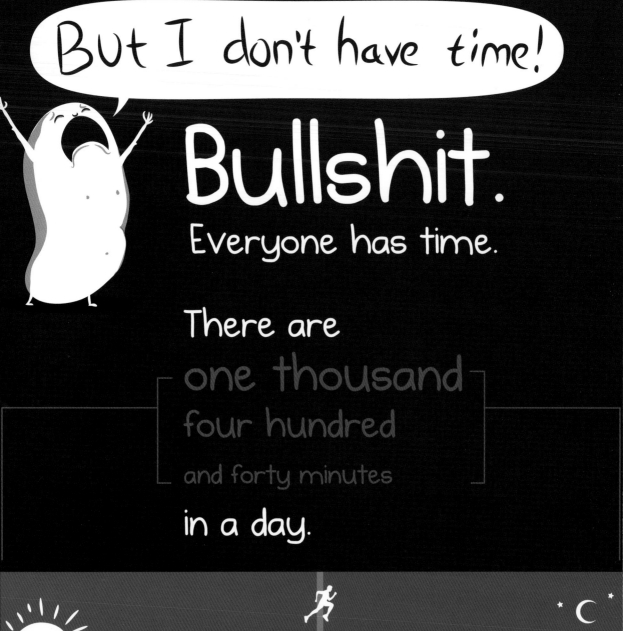

Giving up smoking is hard.

Waking up early is unnatural.

Dieting is frustrating.

Running hurts.

When you combine these goals into a single four-legged beast, all it takes is one of those legs to buckle and everything crashes down.

It is a brittle way of eliciting change.

Instead, craft a beast that sits firmly upon one leg.

Change one habit at a time.

UNSTOPPABLE!

HOP!

HOP!

Otherwise you're just setting yourself up for failure.

It looks like we overslept, Mr. Kitty! Well, our whole plan is now shot. THIS CALLS FOR TACOS AND SCOTCH FOR BREAKFAST!

10:09

CLINK!

I've been running long distances for nearly ten years now, and even *I* don't wake up at 5 am to exercise.
I run when I *need* to, not when I'm *supposed* to, and I don't typically *need* to do anything at 5 am except dream, fart, and sleep.

Many endurance athletes insist on waking up super early to train. I am not one of those athletes.
I'm a runner, not a fucking werewolf.

There is nothing good about 5 am.
In the Bible it clearly states that 5 am is the hour in which Satan gets a big angry demon boner.

5:08

It is a wretched time.
Stay away from it.

3. Remember:

running sucks
in the beginning.

If you've never run farther than a mile in your entire life,
I'm willing to bet you hate running—and understandably so,
you've only experienced the crappy part.

You've never peeked beyond those first few minutes of torment.
You don't know the raging tiki party of bliss that lies beyond.

If you tell a non-runner that you ran a full marathon, all 26.2 miles of it, they'll say something like this:

26.2 miles?! That's 26.2 times harder than running ONE mile! That's incredible! You're incredible!

I'm incredible.

But, as most runners know, this isn't how it works.
It's easier than that. I'm not saying it's *easy*,
I'm simply saying that it's not 26.2 times *harder*.

Running sucks in the beginning. There are burning lungs and tired muscles and heaps of misery and frustration.
But it doesn't stay that way.

It's a front-loaded chore.

Starting out, your body is going to fight you. It's got a vested interest in keeping you fat, comfortable, and warm—and it's going to protect that interest. Whether it's the first few minutes of a run or the first few weeks of training, that hairy meat tricycle of yours is going to give you plenty of reasons to go sit down.

You just have to keep going.
You have to win that argument against your body.

After that you're free.

If you find yourself hating running

and quitting early,

just keep at it.

Running takes time to become enjoyable.
It's not a surgical strike; it's a war of attrition.

And any war that ends with a tiki party is a war worth fighting.

4. Run outside.

If you want to hate running,
I highly recommend using a treadmill.

It's a fun little device. It enables you to sweat in place while
being taunted by a glowing panel of decrementing integers
which maddeningly remind you of how much longer things
are going to suck.

It is like being taunted by a cyborg.
A cyborg never tires.
A cyborg does not know fatigue.
A cyborg knows only
ones and zeros.

RUN FASTER,
FATTY!

Cyborgs are dicks.

If possible, find a loop.

Run in a big, looped course outside,
ideally just beyond the perimeter of your comfort zone.

A treadmill enables you to push a bright red quit button
at any time, but when you run a circular course,
you're *forced* to make the return trip home.

I've noticed that when I run on a
treadmill or an out-and-back course,
I almost always quit early.

Minimize your boredom: run outdoors on a looped course.
You can see the wilderness.
You can see the cityscape.
Maybe you'll see a rainbow.
Maybe you'll see a caribou taking a dump.

Whatever you see,
you'll only have to see it once.

You are mitigating monotony.

Sure, on a treadmill you can distract yourself with music or TV, but I run to get out of the house and *feel* better, not to burn calories while catching up on bad TV.

Running is an accessible sport: all you need is a pair of shoes and a wide, open space. Embrace that accessibility and run outside.

{ I treat a run as if it were a hike. When I go hiking, I have a rough idea of where I'm going and generally how long it's going to take, but I don't dwell on pace, calories, or mileage. I'm not robotically counting my steps and quitting the hike as soon as I hit an arbitrary number. }

I understand that some people simply *can't* run outside.
Certain neighborhoods can be dangerous after dark.
There are muggers and quicksand and vampire bats and whatnot.

But, if a choice exists between a treadmill and the outdoors,
choose the outdoors.

Choose bats, not cyborgs.

5. Sign up for an *event.*

Distance runners are manic beasts.

We often train alone, quietly shuffling along the pavement for hours on end – our only companion being a bottomless well of sweat, pain, and introspection. Even social runners – those who run in a group, often wind up drifting out of the pack and plodding along quietly at their own pace.

To a bystander, we may appear sullen or lonely,

and maybe we are.

But on race day, that all changes.

A marathon is the collective release of thousands of hours of solitary tedium taking the form of a massive crowd of strangers all choosing to hurt themselves in exactly the same way.

ow OUCH ow ow ow ow ouch I'M SAD OW ow OW ow
arg DON'T CRAMP NOW goddamnit FOR NO REASON! ouch ouch owowow OW
I HATE THIS ow ow ow ow ack ow ow ow ow ooh agh arg ow OW ow I NEED A TOILET ARG SERIOUSLY, oooh ow
ow MY ASS! OH GOD MY ASS! WHY THE F☆☆ BOOB CHAFING? shit

It's wonderful. Or awful.
It's both, really.
The entire spectrum of human emotion
is at play during a marathon.

It's an experience that's hard to put into words.

The closest comparison I can think of is if ten thousand pregnant ladies all met in the street and started firing infants out of their hoo-haws in a massive game of amniotic paintball.

It would be a messy ordeal.

There would be sweat.
There would be tears.
There would be police cars and barricades.

But in the end, an army of countless baby-people would emerge, all feasting on orange slices and high-fiving one another for a job well done.

I AM EUPHORIC AND SWEATY!

I AM A JOYFUL MAN WITH CHAFED TESTICLES!

SLAP!

I'm not sure this analogy makes sense.

FORGET THE BABIES.

What I'm trying to say is this:

Running a race assigns a POINT to a sport that often feels very POINTLESS.

It's an **exuberant payoff** to months of tedium.

It's a way of crafting an **end boss** for a particularly cumbersome video game.

It's a fun, monstrous reason to keep putting one foot in front of the other.

So, do yourself a favor: go build a monster.

Sign up for a race.

26.2

6. Don't think ahead.

I've spent most of my life living fifteen minutes in the future. If I'm at a restaurant enjoying a tasty beer, my mind is focused on the meal I just ordered. If I'm eating that meal, I'm thinking about dessert. If I'm eating dessert, I'm thinking about catching a movie after dinner.

I'm never *present* — I'm dwelling on the next *exciting-fun-treat* that's headed my way.

Running hurts.

Running will *always* hurt. You do get used to it, and the pain certainly diminishes, but there's always a certain degree of suffering.

I work very hard to *own* this suffering. Much like eating, I try to NOT live in the future. I don't dwell on my next reward and count the seconds until my next awesome-special-feel-good-surprise.

I possess my circumstances,
whether they're terrible, wonderful, or somewhere in between.

I've adopted a little mantra that sometimes helps:

Yes, this hurts. And it's going to continue to hurt. And that's okay.

Yes, this is tasty. And it's going to continue to be tasty. And that's okay.

3601

Meaty LARD CAKES
SO MUCH YUM!

Some people choose NOT to cope with the tedium and pain of running, and instead distract themselves by listening to music or chatting with other runners. This can help pass the time, but it also waters down the core of what it takes to be a distance runner.

Running is a form of

practiced stoicism.

It means teaching your brain and body to be biomechanically comfortable in a state of disrepair.

Distractions enable you to *put off* that discomfort — to procrastinate confronting an inexorable march of pain.

But pain and hardship are neither friend nor foe to a runner: they're neighbors.

They're familiar. A known quantity.

7. Become a *drug addict.*

I eat too much. I always have.

And I eat too fast. Food is not delicately placed into my face; it is *shoveled*. I eat snacks like I'm burying bodies in the dark: it's frantic and shameful and it frightens the neighbors.

And after 30+ years of overeating, I've taken a hard look at why I do this, and I've come to an understanding:

I overeat because food *tastes* good, but more importantly, I do it because it *feels* good.

It's a nine minute vacation.

It's a short dip into a shallow pool of chewing, tasting, and swallowing.

It's an escape for a greedy, fat, impulsive man-child who happens to be wearing grown-up clothes.

nutella

I often regard overeating as a drug addiction,

and I try to imagine what my life would be like if that addiction got the best of me. I picture the years wearing on, with earth's annual trip around the sun being marked by an increase in pant sizes and a decrease in self worth. I imagine my heart getting tighter and more flustered, until one sunny morning it shudders to a violent halt. I imagine myself wrenching forward, my face heaving into a pile of waffles. I imagine my last breath gurgling into a tepid pool of maple syrup.

I imagine all of these things, and I think:

I don't want to die face-first in a pile of waffles.

I want to die in an electrical storm.
I want to die wrestling a Kodiak bear.
I want to die in an EXPLOSION.

I want to die quietly at home,
hand in hand with somebody who loved me.

I just don't want to die by waffles. Anything but waffles.

Here lies
Matthew Inman.
He REALLY liked
waffles.

And so,

motivated by fear,

I choose to be a different kind of drug addict:

I choose to be a runner.

And make no mistake: running *is* an addiction, both chemically and spiritually. There are euphoric highs, terrible lows, and the constant desire to "squeeze in a quick run" in order to feel whole.

But unlike other drug addictions, running is *socially acceptable.* It's like being able to smoke crack every day, but instead of getting strung out and arrested you get bananas and compliments.

And it's certainly more socially acceptable than dieting.

Being a former fat kid was a motivator as well,

and I've often wondered it if was a blessing or a curse.
It turned me into an active, health-conscious adult, but I also
live with the daily fear that I'm on the verge of turning back
into a chubby little sad-monster.

Even now, decades later, I'm still convinced that I'm only a
few meals away from becoming Mr. Hyde with love handles.

It's a stupid, pointless worry,
but it's a worry that's here to stay.

So, to cope with that stupidity, I started running, and I eventually came to a point where something "broke" in my head. A *reversal* occurred, and it became more painful for me to remain sedentary than to be active.

I figured out that it hurt more to feel fat and depressed than to put on a pair of running shoes and log a few more miles in hell.

It's a nice place to be, I suppose,
this deranged little fitness nirvana, wherein the pain of depression outweighs the pain of physical torment.

Is this a healthy, responsible way to live?
Fuck it. Who cares.

It's better than the waffles.

8. Hurt yourself today.

I am neither old nor wise, but I have learned some things.
I've learned that sometimes if I'm having an awesome day,

hurt and awfulness

like to rain down from the sky
and hit me right in my jolly little face.

That's just life.
Sometimes good things happen and
sometimes bad things happen. I'm not in control.

I'm just a jellyfish riding the tormented swells
of a violent, uncaring ocean.

But when I run, *I* control the hurt.

It's a form of hurt I can *possess*.

There's an enduring myth that distance runners are impervious to pain — that we're a bunch of freakish stoics who are immune to physical stress. This is not true. Runners aren't impervious to pain, we're just better at *choosing* what kind of pain we have to feel.

And when I run, that's exactly what I'm doing.

I'm asserting control over the uncontrollable.

I'm housebreaking a tornado.

Running is a way of standing up to all the
stupid shit in your life and saying:
*I don't know how to fix you,
so I'll just bend you into workable shapes.*

And the day I put on a pair of running shoes,
I did just that.

I chose *not* to combat my monsters,
I chose to put them on a leash
and take them for a walk instead.

I chose *not* to fix my torment.
I chose to own it.

To possess it.

I chose to
RUN.

The End.

Notes & acknowledgments

The hornet/lightning run:

My crazy bamboo-lightning run happened in the Meitoku neighborhood of Nagoya, Japan, and as far as I know that purple drink is still in those vending machines (although still heavily guarded by winged, nightmare insects).

"I run to seek a void."

This line was paraphrased from *What I Talk About When I Talk About Running*, a wonderful book by Haruki Murakami.

My favorite runs in Seattle:

If I'm looking to just clock some easy miles, I run around Green Lake or on the Burke-Gilman Trail. If I'm looking for hills, I run at Discovery Park. If I'm looking for scenic, well-marked trails, I run at Cougar Mountain. If I'm looking to get stung by nettles and chased by bears, I run at Tiger Mountain. If I'm looking to get accosted by crackheads and pooped on by seagulls, I run downtown.

My favorite distance: Half marathon.

My favorite mid-run snack: Japanese o'nigiri.

My PRs: I run often but I am by no means an impressive runner. I once ran a half marathon in one hour and thirty minutes, and I can *sometimes* run a sub-six-minute mile, but that's about as competitive as I get.

I am much more competitive when it comes to eating and napping, so if these activities are added to the Olympics, please let me know because I will be crowned champ of champs.

About the author

This book was written and drawn by
Matthew Inman,

AKA *The Oatmeal.*

Matthew lives in Seattle, Washington, with his two overweight, poorly behaved dogs, Rambo and Beatrix.

Visit www.theoatmeal.com for more of Matthew's comics, or check out his other books:

→ How to Tell If Your Cat Is Plotting to Kill You

→ My Dog: The Paradox

→ Why Grizzly Bears Should Wear Underpants

→ 5 Very Good Reasons to Punch a Dolphin in the Mouth

THE TERRIBLE AND WONDERFUL REASONS
WHY I RUN LONG DISTANCES

copyright © 2014 by Oatmeal, LLC. All rights reserved. Printed in China. No part of this book
may be used or reproduced in any manner whatsoever without written permission except in the
case of reprints in the context of reviews.

Andrews McMeel Publishing, LLC
an Andrews McMeel Universal company
1130 Walnut Street, Kansas City, Missouri 64106

www.andrewsmcmeel.com

14 15 16 17 18 TEN 10 9 8 7 6 5 4 3 2 1

ISBN: 978-1-4494-5995-6

Library of Congress Control Number: 2014937161

ATTENTION: SCHOOLS AND BUSINESSES
Andrews McMeel books are available at quantity discounts with bulk purchase for
educational, business, or sales promotional use. For information, please e-mail the
Andrews McMeel Publishing Special Sales Department: specialsales@amuniversal.com.